In the same series:
Love, a celebration (1981)
Marriage, a keepsake (1982)
For Mother, a gift of love (1983)
For Grandad, a gift of love (1983)

Also edited by Helen Exley:
Grandmas and Grandpas (1975)
To Mum (1976)
To Dad (1976)
Happy Families (1977)
What is a Husband? (1977)
Cats (and other crazy cuddlies) (1978)
Dogs (and other funny furries) (1978)
Dear World (1978)
A Child's View of Happiness (1979)
A Child's View of Christmas (1980)
What is a Baby? (1980)
What it's like to be me (1981)
What is a Wife? (1982)
A Gift of Flowers (1983)

Published by Exley Publications Ltd, 16 Chalk Hill,
Watford, Herts, United Kingdom WD1 4BN
Selection and design © Exley Publications Ltd 1983
First published in Great Britain 1983

Printed in Great Britain by Butler & Tanner Ltd, Frome

British Library Cataloguing in Publication Data
Love is grandmother.
   1. Grandmothers – Literary collections
   I. Exley, Helen
   820.8'0352'0432   PR1111.G/

   ISBN 0-905521-92-7

Love is a
GRANDMOTHER

Edited by Helen Exley

HOW TO TELL IF SHE'S A GRAN.

Grandmas sometimes race you to the next lamp post . . .but then they sit on a wall, and go a funny colour.

Grandchildren explore your face as if it were a treasure map, greeting every discovery with enthusiasm – moles, whiskers, wrinkles, gold filled teeth. Nice to know it's all been worthwhile to someone!

The most maddening thing about grans is that they don't *use* the presents you give them. They even keep the ribbon.

Grandmas don't just say 'that's nice' – they reel back and roll their eyes and throw up their hands and smile. You get your money's worth out of grans.

Sampler based on a design in 'The Family Circle'

To become a grandmother is a mixture of joy and indignation.

Never ask a grandma a favour till she's had a cup of tea.

Every mother smiles 'how *clever* I am' – but the years with the mistakes and regrets and anxieties dim the glory. Till the first grandchild – a sort of second chance, that wipes out all the blunders.

Upstretched arms make grandmas put off rheumatism till tomorrow.

It takes a lifetime to get back to knowing you don't know anything: that's why grandmothers and grandchildren get on so well together.

Of course, there *are* grandmas that believe in Clean Clothes and Sitting Up To Table – but they don't get asked round too often.

It is remarkable how, overnight, a fat elderly lady can learn to sit cross legged on the floor and play a tin drum, quack like a duck, sing all the verses of 'The Twelve Days of Christmas', make paper flowers, draw pigs and sew on the ears of severely injured teddy bears.

A GRANDMOTHER IS . . .

Grandmothers walk slowly and so rediscover petrol rainbows, fallen leaves, puddles and worms in need of rescue.

The girl I always have been looks out bewildered at this little child who calls me grandma.

Grandmothers have old feet and young hearts.

Grans share a child's vision of the world. The child is meeting things for the first time. Grans are beginning to say goodbye.

In their bags grans have sweeties, loo paper, aspirin, scissors, needle and thread, vaseline, sellotape, Bandaids, a police whistle, three combs, six ballpoints and a pencil, a penknife, a spoon, a clump of safety pins, another bag of sweeties, a length of string, four elastic bands, a diary, an address book, a packet of postcards, six stamps with no sticky, a tube of paper paste, a pension book and an Agatha Christie.

One would be a little shocked to know the details of one's mother's youth – but in grandmothers one can forgive *anything*.

Some mums are very ambitious for their children. Most grans just want the children to be happy – they've discovered for themselves just how little time everyone has.

Mothers plan and arrange and decide: grans watch the little child move into new life, knowing that for all the plans and all the love it must blunder and fall as we have done.

Grandmas are *always* astonished to find themselves old enough to be grandmas.

Pam Brown

WHAT IS A GRANDMOTHER?

A grandmother is a lady who has no children of her own, so she likes other people's little girls and boys. A grandfather is a man grandmother. He goes for walks with the boys and they talk about fishing and tractors.

Grandmothers don't have to do anything but be there. They are old so they shouldn't play hard or run. They should never say, 'Hurry up'. Usually they are fat, but not too fat to tie children's shoes.

They wear glasses and funny underwear, and they can take their teeth and gums off.

They don't have to be smart, only answer questions, like why dogs hate cats and why God isn't married. They don't talk baby-talk like visitors. When they read to us, they don't skip bits, or mind if it is the same story over again.

Everybody should have one, especially if you don't have television, because grandmothers are the only grown-ups who have the time!

Patsy Gray, aged 7

There's something engaging
about the combination of very young people
and very mature people.
A child challenges most parents
to be stable and responsible.
A grandchild challenges the grandparent
to put aside all that stuff
and have fun.

Charles and Ann Morse

The oddities of shape that age has given me,
defeating exercise and diet,
making me appear hump-backed, pot-bellied,
    flabby-armed
when inside in reality I am slim and straight
and, bracing all my muscles,
prove to be purpose-built
for carting grandchildren from place to place.
I am a breathing, ambulatory armchair
the perfect place for cuddles.

Pamela Brown

Top of the Pops charts for Christmas 1981:-
from THERE'S NO ONE QUITE LIKE
GRANDMA

Grandma, we love you
Grandma, we do.
Though you may be far away, we think of you.
There's no one quite like Grandma and I know you
    will agree
She always is a friend to you,
And she's a friend to me,
There's no one quite like Grandma,
She's there in times of need
Before it's bedtime on her knee,
To us a book she'll read.

Grandma, we love you, Grandma, we do
Though you may be far away, we think of you
And one day, when we're older
We'll look back and say
There's no one quite like Grandma,
She has helped us on our way.

Gordon Lorenz

HEATH
A LONG WAY
AFTER
GILES

GRANNY-POWER

Some of the best people are becoming grannies
these days. And I shouldn't be surprised if
grandmotherhood suddenly catches on like punk
rock.

This new surge of granny-power could be very
good news because a good granny can boost your
confidence more than a chorus of wolf-whistles
when you haven't got lipstick on.

A good granny clucks over your carry-cot the
minute you're born and says: 'Well, I never did.
This is the most beautiful baby I've ever seen in my
life – and I'm not prejudiced.'

Then she turns to your Mum and goes on: 'Mind
you, I'm not surprised. Seeing how our side of the
family have always had the reputation for being
gorgeous.'

When you make her an Easter card at nursery
school, she keeps it in her handbag and fishes it out
to show her friends, and the nice woman standing
beside her in the bus queue.

Then she sticks it in a scrapbook, together with one of your baby curls, and an item in the local paper announcing that you came third in the fancy-dress competition organized by the Junior Chamber of Commerce.

When you're top of the class, she gives you a quid and a kiss and tells everyone: 'You wouldn't think that anyone as clever as my little granddaughter could be so beautiful, too.'

But if your school report says, 'Must try harder,' she says: 'Never mind, ducks. Look at Winston Churchill. He never did himself justice at school, and neither did your Uncle Fred – and look where he is now. If you want my opinion, those clever dicks who pass exams burn themselves out before they've begun – and that's a fact.'

When your Mum says, 'What do you think you're playing at sitting down at the table with a mucky face,' your granny murmurs: 'It's only *clean* dirt.'

When your Dad takes one look at your lurex ankle socks and Afghan jerkin and says, 'You're not going out like that, are you?' your granny says: 'Well I think she looks a picture.'

And, on your wedding day, she takes your brand-new husband aside, puts a little wrinkled hand on his arm and hisses in his ear: 'You're a very lucky lad. That girl could have had her pick, you know.'   ▷

Even though it was you who had your work cut out catching *him*.

Sadly, some grannies never acquire this knack of making you feel that you did the world a big favour by getting yourself born.

In fact, a ghastly granny can make you wish that the wolf in Red Riding Hood would hurtle through the window and wrap his choppers around her neck.

When you have lunch with a ghastly granny, she gives you boiled cod and watery cabbage and stands over you, while you push it around your plate, saying: 'None of my children were allowed to be fussy eaters.'

When your Mum comes to collect you, your granny says: 'Of course, in my day, children were

potty-trained by the time they were one-year-old, and never answered back.

'But, of course, mothers in those days were prepared to make a few sacrifices for their family and not go gadding about all over the place.'

Or they're so horrified at being made a granny at all that they put up a desperate fight against the situation.

They arrive at your christening with strawberry-blonde curls and a jump suit, and, after too many sweet sherries, lurch around saying: 'I expect you're amazed that I'm the grandma. But I was a child bride.'

Even when you're old enough to introduce them to your boyfriend, they waggle their bright blue lashes at him and say: 'I hope you're going to call me Thelma, because I just know that we're going to be friends.'

Which makes his ears turn a fiery scarlet.

My own granny is definitely The Greatest. And I think that anybody else's granny, even if she happens to live at Buckingham Palace, will have to put in a bit of overtime if she wants to wrest the title away from her.

Just to start with, she'll have to be prepared to offer cups of tea and a slice of vanilla sponge at any hour of the day or night. And ring up at seven in the morning just to tell you that she loves you.

Penny Perrick

Who went into mild hysterics when told the news?

Who suffered nine months of waiting, wondering
and secretly agonising?

Who waited for twelve hours by the phone waiting
for news?

Who rushed off to the hospital babbling like an
idiot?

Who bawled like a baby when shown him?

Who's the proudest and daftest person when he's
around?

Who shows him off like some priceless jewel?

Who? Me, Mark's very lucky grandma.

L. Milnes

I had forgotten how beautiful a newborn baby is. It is a myth that all babies look alike. Some newborn babies are red and scrawny and squally; others are pink and cuddly and cute. I suppose you think that, as a grandmother, I might be prejudiced about this particular baby, but my years as a journalist have made it possible for me to observe objectively, and in so doing, I have to admit that Joshua Lee Bloomingdale, at age fifty-three minutes, was the most beautiful baby God ever created.

Teresa Bloomingdale

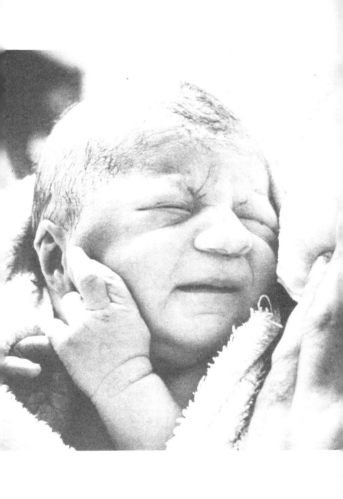

My baby daughter arrived, and brought with her –
immortality! No longer was I one person. I was two
persons, with the glorious possibility of being a part
of any number of persons in the future.

My ideas; my moral standards; my oddities and
idiosyncrasies; my love of books and games; my
horror of mice; my inability to do the simplest
sums; the awkward surge of emotion that
overcomes me when I see human goodness – some
part of me had a chance of living after me, and even
spreading – so that there might be a bit of me in the
world for a long time to come! I liked the idea.

It may sound a bit self-satisfied, but I hope my
daughter and now my beloved granddaughter, 'the
pulse and core of my heart', (as the Irish say) have
not learned or inherited anything really *bad* from
me. I may have spoiled them a bit, but only with
love, and I don't believe *real* love does any harm.
(Real love can be very tough.) And how bare my life
would have been without them. I'm an old woman
now, and can go off happily into the unknown sure
that there's a lot of me left behind.

Emily Worthington

I'M NOT A 'PROPER' GRAN

It was, of course, a very proud moment indeed for the lovely, blonde and still girlish Mrs Patricia D'Amico, 36, when she was voted Britain's Most Glamorous Granny.

Patricia, who has four children, has a granddaughter called Danielle.

Danielle at fifteen months, is a bit too young to express views about her gorgeous grandma. But other small grandchildren I know have very decided views indeed about grannies.

Mine, for example. Aged six and five, they call me Dolly and refuse to accept that I am their granny. 'You're not,' said the six-year-old boy firmly when I assured him I was.

Their fixed notion of a granny is an elderly, cosy lady, with white hair and a soft capacious bosom who sits by the fire, knitting.

'Grannies,' say my two, 'don't go out to work and listen to pop music and drive cars and wear trousers.'

I have given up trying to convince them that all

grannies aren't like Little Red Riding Hood's, reckoning it's best to leave them with their granny-image intact for the time being.

Mrs D'Amico will probably face a similar problem when Danielle begins to ask questions. For the truth is that, while glamorous grandmas can congratulate themselves on looking so young, what their children's children expect are grannies who fit the storybook image.

They like grannies with large snuggly bosoms who make them feel safe and warm. They love to hear stories about the 'old days'.

They're mad about old-fashioned photos of ladies in old-fashioned clothes and listening to quaint old-fashioned songs like 'Daisy, Daisy'. 'Jail House Rock' isn't their idea of the granny scene. All this poses a dilemma for grandmothers. Should they knock themselves out to stay young and trendy, watch their weight and go easy on the make-up as Mrs D'Amico advises? Which is very nice indeed for grandads.

Or should they let it all go and stop tinting their hair and half-starving themselves and grow plump in order to provide their grandchildren with the cosy reassurance which, traditionally, they expect?

Remembering my own lovely white-haired gran, I wonder if I'm depriving my two by being merely 'Dolly'.

Marje Proops

GRANDMOTHERS' LIBERATION

Perhaps the physical care of grandchildren is so exhausting because one is so anxious to be popular with them, to win their love, and to make sure that they like being with you better than with the other grandmother. The child's mother will naturally say, 'Run away and play – I'm busy,' whereas the grandmother reads aloud until she is hoarse, or sits uncomfortably on the floor, making a station for the toy train out of a box. To be indulgent is a great temptation. But to be indulgent with grandchildren is to be *self*-indulgent, to place popularity and love above what one knows is better for their character.

I am very proud of having grandchildren and I show off their pictures, just like any other grandmother. But I am not going to re-live all my past experiences; I am going forward with new ones of my own. I am rediscovering the pleasure of being able to devote myself to my husband after so many years of divided attention. This is our time for growing in our own way – and not for depending on our grandchildren to give us a new lease of life.

Lucy Worcester, from
'A Grandmother Grows Up'

WHAT IS A GRANDMOTHER?

A grandmother is a little girl who suddenly shows up one day with a touch of grey in her hair.

Better than anything, she has a way of understanding little boys. Especially men who are grown-up little boys.

Something about a grandmother is always making you hungry. Maybe it's the apple pies baking and the chicken frying and the biscuits in the oven. But Grandma always has the nicest smelling house.

Long before Band-Aids were invented, she was the best person to take care of scraped knees and scratched elbows and banged heads. It was something in the way she touched you.

Grandmother was an expert on mischief, too. Especially when you had been into it. When she looked right into your eyes it was pretty hard to fool her about what really happened. Really.

And it was when you were almost too big to sit in her lap that you began to learn that she was a very special person to talk to. Sometimes, she would give you the right answers without ever saying a word.

How did a little girl ever grow up to be so clever? Maybe it came with the grey hair. Maybe it came suddenly with being a grandmother.

Harry McMahan

ORDERS OF THE DAY

Get up!
Get washed!
Eat your breakfast!
That's my mum,
Going on and on and on and on and on . . .

Sit down!
Shut up!
Get on with your work!!
That's my teacher,
Going on and on and on and on and on . . .

Come here!
Give me that!
That's my big sister,
Going on and on and on and on and on . . .

Get off!
Stop it!
Carry me!
That's my little sister,
Going on and on and on and on and on . . .

Boss
Boss
Boss
They do it all day.
Sometimes I think I'll run away,
But I don't know
Where to go.

The only one who doesn't do it,
Is my old gran.
She says,
'Would you like to get washed?'
Or,
'Would you like to sit on this chair?'
And she listens to what I say.

People say she spoils me,
And that she's old-fashioned.
I think it's the others that spoil;
Spoil every day.
And I wish more people were old-fashioned,
. . . like my gran.

John Cunliffe

I know a little cupboard
With a teeny tiny key
And there's a jar of Lollipops
    For me, me, me .

It has a little shelf, my dear,
As dark as dark can be,
And there's a dish of Banbury Cakes
    For me, me, me.

I have a small fat grandmama
With a very slippery knee,
And she's Keeper of the Cupboard
    With the key, key, key.

And when I'm very good, my dear,
As good as good can be
There's Banbury Cakes, and Lollipops
  For me, me, me.

Walter De la Mare

GRAN COMES WEDNESDAYS

Gran comes dragged down with bags,
hair all awry,
Clean out of breath from puffing up the road.
She sits and sags
till Mum has stoked her up with tea,
and I sit on her knee
and struggle not to pry
into that interesting load
until she gives the word.
One bulge is bound to be for me
for Mum gets tins
and Dad gets two or three
posh motor magazines
she's given where she cleans,
but I get special things
like buttons, coloured beads,
bottles that smell of scent,
a bird
all stuck with sequins,
rings
with diamonds big as peas,
and, once, a bear
that, as Gran says,
has personality –
and seeds
to sow behind the garden shed.

She brings nice presents
does my Gran
And likes to come to see
my rabbit
and the frog I found that's dead
and stays
to read a story
when I go to bed.

Pam Brown

A VISIT TO GRANNIE

I love to sit and chat to her
– Her old wise head
Nodding and clicking
Bone on bone . . . . . .

Swinging my bag at
Each leap of the
Churchyard stones,
Banging the door
Of the family tomb
– I've jerked her awake again
But she never complains –
Kissing her dear dead yawn.

I open my bag and pour out
What I've brought her
– The latest neurosis,
An ultra modern grievance –
And the light peeks through
Those honest eyes,
Through her kindly smiling jaw.

When I come away
I always feel better:
Grannie, you're so much wiser
Than we are.

Elizabeth Maslen

OLD MRS BODFAN'S DANCE

Oh! Crikey. O, Oh! Crikey-O,
I smell the spring today.
I smell the earth,
I hear buds burst,
I feel the roots begin to stir.
The birds are singing in the hedge
and soft air turns my vane.
Everywhere I look are signs
that spring is here again.

Oh! Crikey-O, Oh! Crikey-O,
no spring is in my bones
not in my face,
not in my hair,
not in my step or stoop.
Yet I must give a *little* leap
in welcome to the spring,
and thank the Lord who's let me live
to see this season in.

Kusha Petts

GRANDMAMA'S BIRTHDAY

Dear Grandmama, with what we give,
We humbly pray that you may live
For many, many happy years:
Although you bore us all to tears.

Hilaire Belloc

BABBLING AND GABBLING

My Granny's an absolute corker,
My Granny's an absolute cracker,
But she's Britain's speediest talker
And champion yackety-yacker!

Everyone's fond of my Granny,
Everyone thinks she's nice,
But before you can say Jack Robinson,
My Granny's said it twice!

Kit Wright

The odd antics of merry widow Jennie Gorman have got her barred from a nightclub.

For right in the middle of a comedy act at the club, she got up from the audience and insisted on showing off her dancing outfit. She unzipped her purple evening gown to reveal red hot pants, fishnet stockings and garters. And emblazoned on her chest was a saucy 'I'm A Virgin' badge.

It was all too much for Derek Kirkbride, manager of the club, the Rendezvous in Workington, Cumberland. He reckoned that Jennie had gone too far – it was no way for a *seventy-four*-year-old granny to behave.

He said: 'It wasn't the sort of display we want in this club. I told her never to come in here again. She is known in another club in the town for go-go dancing in her hot pants, but she's never dared to do it in our place before.'

Unrepentant Jennie, of Headlands Crescent, Workington, said: 'I just wanted to liven things up. I've become quite a merry widow since losing my husband five years ago. I like to live it up by going go-go dancing. I bought my hot pants at a sale and sewed on the badge.

'Too old at 74? Not a bit of it. I'm just beginning to live.'

Sydney Foxcroft, from a newscutting in the 'Sunday People'

In love with his neighbour's daughter, Mr Dorsun Yilmaz of Dalmali, Yugoslavia, organized an elopement.

Soon after midnight, his beloved, wrapped in a blanket, descended the ladder he had placed by her window. He carried her to the car and away they sped.

Five miles down the road he unwrapped his treasure, and found that he was carrying the girl's grandmother, who beat him up.

The Sun, 26 August 1972

A debutante went to visit her grandmother. The old lady was distressed by what she considered the girl's wild and slangy speech. She decided she must reprimand her granddaughter.

One evening she said gently, 'Dear, there are just two words I want you to refrain from using. One is 'swell' and the other is 'lousy'.'

'All right,' replied the debutante agreeably. 'What are they?'

Michael Aspel

GRANDMA GOES TO A PARTY

I would unzip my skin
and hang it on a chair,
take off this wig,
let down my yellow hair
and dance until the dawn
. . . if I could break the spell
that trickster time has played.
But all the words are lost.
This wearisome charade
must go on as before.
I watch the children spin.
And sigh. And yawn.

Pam Brown

A KIND OF EQUALITY

An interesting point about grandmothers generally
is that they are not usually seen as disciplinarians
but as indulgers of children. Anthropologists call
this the 'equivalence of generations'; that is,
alternate generations are structurally equal, and can
therefore behave towards each other in a more
relaxed way than can consecutive generations. In
Guiana, too, there is a normal grandchild-
grandparent relationship of this kind, which is one
of 'affectionate indulgence, and a kind of equality'.
A grandmother often identifies with her
grandchildren and takes their side in quarrels with
the mother. When a young girl wants to go to a
dance, and has been forbidden by her mother, the
grandmother may plead for her.

Grandparents and grandchildren can joke with
each other in a way which is often impossible for
parents and children to do. Grandchildren can tease
or even disobey their grandparents without
meriting punishment. Perhaps this is why
grandmothers often say they can 'enjoy' their
grandchildren more than they ever could their own
children. The grandmother does not have to justify
her right to be a mother or prove her ability to rear
the baby and can see the problems of crises of
family life in perspective from the vantage point of

experience. She can relax and enjoy the child.
   Grandmothers often criticize their
daughters-in-law for punishments which they
consider too harsh, even though they may have
punished their own children in a similar way.

Sheila Kitzinger

from 'GRANDMOTHER EXTRAORDINARY'

Her exploits excited a variety of reactions among
family and friends at home. Attitudes ranged from
admiration to incredulity, amazement was mixed
with amused tolerance. But from one generation of
the Nicholl family she knew only unreserved
affection, tinged with adulation. Her grandchildren
were devoted to her. She, who as a young mother
had felt a certain estrangement from her own
children, discovered in her grandchildren a
never-ending source of pleasure. And they, in their
turn, adored her. For Grandmama knew so much
about everything. From her they learnt the names
of the flowers and trees, how to identify the birds
and the butterflies, and country walks with
Grandmama were a constant delight. And unlike
most grown-ups she was an enthusiastic supporter
of such activities as tree-climbing and rock-
climbing, her own pleasure rivalling that of
her grandchildren when any of them showed the
same fearless courage and instinctive climbing
prowess that she herself had possessed. And then
there was Grandmama's marvellous repertoire of
stories that never palled in the repeated telling, tales
of her own adventures and tales of her imagination
that held her young audience spell-bound.

It is in the memories of her grandchildren that
Mary De la Beche Nicholl still lives today. Some

were fortunate enough to accompany Grandmama on her travels, and have left their own descriptions of the events of those travels. Gwennie (later Lyon) went with her grandmother to the Gredos Mountains of Spain and experienced at first hand the adventure of tents, camps under the stars, donkey and horse rides, and the inevitable butterfly hunts. Members of the Nicholl family still recall with amused affection a letter from Gwennie describing her Spanish travels and recounting how Grandmama was received by the mayor and band of one remote Spanish village and conducted with great ceremony to the town hall. Minnie had been mistaken for Queen Victoria! And there are other grandchildren alive today who can still recall with unclouded memory and unreserved affection the fascinating person who was Grandmama.

Hilary M. Thomas, from 'Grandmother Extraordinary'

WHEN I LOOK IN YOUR EYES

This is my favourite song — of all the ones I sing.
I think of my grandmother whenever I sing it.

Frankie Vaughan

When I look in your eyes
I see the wisdom of the world in your eyes,
I see the sadness of a thousand goodbyes
When I look in your eyes
. . . Autumn comes, summer dies,
I see the passing of the years in your eyes,
And when we part there'll be no tears, no
    goodbyes,
I'll just look into your eyes.
Those eyes so wise, so warm, so real,
How I love the world your eyes reveal.

Leslie Bricusse

Other gift books produced by Exley Publications

For Grandad, a gift of love, £4.95. A companion collection to this volume, bound in chocolate brown suedel. Writers include George Bernard Shaw, Ogden Nash, Roger McGough, Margaret Mead and Mike Harding. Giftwrapped with sealing wax.

Love, a Celebration, £4.95. In the same series as this but with a burgundy suedel cover. Writers and poets old and new have captured the feeling of being in love, in this very personal collection. Gift wrapped with sealing wax. Give it to someone special.

Marriage, a Keepsake, £4.95. Also in the same series, but with a dove-grey suedel cover. This collection of poems and prose celebrates marriage with some of the finest love messages between husbands and wives. A gift for all ages – from those about to be married to those who have known fifty good years and more together. Giftwrapped with sealing wax.

For Mother, a gift of love, £4.95. This collection of tributes to mothers is bound in pale blue suedel. Rudyard Kipling, Noël Coward, T. B. Macaulay, Victor Hugo, Norman Mailer, C. Day Lewis and Alfred Lord Tennyson are among the contributors. Giftwrapped with sealing wax.

Grandmas & Grandpas, £3.95. Children are close to grandparents, and this book reflects that warmth. 'A Grandma is old on the outside and young on the inside.' An endearing book for grandparents.

To Dad, £3.95. 'Fathers are always right, and even if they're not right, they're never actually wrong.' Dads will love this book – it's so true to life! A regular favourite.

What is a Baby?, £3.95. Parents and grandparents describe the fun and traumas of bringing up baby. A hilarious and beautiful book for any young mother, stunningly illustrated with beautiful photographs.

What is a Husband?, £3.95. 7,500 real wives attempted to answer the question, and the best quotes are here. Pithy, beautiful, hilarious, sad, romantic – all you might expect. Buy a copy for your anniversary!

Simply order through your bookshop, or by post from Exley Publications Ltd., Dept GM, 16 Chalk Hill, Watford, Herts WD1 4BN. Please add 50p per book as a contribution to postage and packing.

permission of the author; LUCY WORCESTER, excerpt from *Vassar Alumnae Magazine*. Reprinted by permission of Vassar Quarterly; KIT WRIGHT, 'Babbling & Gabbling' from *Hot Dog and Other Poems* published by Kestrel Books Ltd. Reprinted by permission of Penguin Books Ltd.

PHOTOGRAPHS AND ILLUSTRATIONS:
BARNABY'S PICTURE LIBRARY: illustrating 'In Memory of Mainie Jellett'; BBC HULTON PICTURE LIBRARY: illustrating 'Looking Back'; CELIA BERRIDGE: illustrating 'The oddities of shape . . .' From *Grandmother's Tales* published by André Deutsch; FRANCES BERRILL: illustrating 'Cowslips'; DAILY MIRROR NEWSPAPER LTD: illustrating 'There's No-one Quite Like Grandma'; JOHN DOIDGE: illustrating 'What is a Grandmother?' and 'To become a grandmother is . . .'; JOHN EDWARDS: illustrating 'There's something engaging about . . .'; RICHARD EXLEY: illustrating 'Gran Comes Wednesdays', 'A Kind of Equality', first pages of 'In pre-industrial societies . . .', 'I Know a Little Cupboard', 'Old Woman' and 'Grandmothers' Liberation'; FOX PHOTOS LTD: illustrating 'Old Mrs Bodfan's Dance'; HEATH: illustrating first two pages of 'Granny-Power'. Reprinted by permission of London Express News and Feature Services; TRINA SCHART HYMAN: illustrating 'A Visit to Grannie'. Reprinted by permission of E.P. Dutton, Inc.; SYLVESTER JACOBS: illustrating 'Grandparents are to be thanked . . .' and 'My baby daughter arrived . . .'; CAMILLA JESSEL: illustrating 'I had forgotten how beautiful . . .'; KEYSTONE PRESS AGENCY LIMITED: illustrating song by Leslie Bricusse; LONDON EXPRESS NEWS AND FEATURES: cartoon by Dominic Poelsma illustrating 'I'm not a 'Proper' Gran'; MARY EVANS PICTURE LIBRARY: illustrating last two pages of 'Granny-Power'; DORKA RAYNOR: illustrating last two pages of Kitzinger's 'In pre-industrial societies . . .', 'Grandchild' and 'Who went into mild hysterics . . .'; SYNDICATION INTERNATIONAL: cartoon illustrating 'A grandmother is . . .'; TROG: illustrating 'Grandma goes to a Party'. Reprinted by permission of Council & Care for the Elderly; JOHN WALMSLEY: illustrating 'I can Answer "Yes" '. From *Waiting for the Dark* by Leila Berg and John Walmsley. Published by Macmillan Education; GEORGE WEDDING: illustrating 'Grandmama's Birthday'. From *The Palm Beach Post*.

ACKNOWLEDGEMENTS: The publishers gratefully acknowledge permission to reproduce copyright material. Every effort has been made to trace copyright holders, but in a few cases this has proved impossible. The publishers would be interested to hear from any copyright holders not here acknowledged.

MICHAEL ASPEL, quote from *Just Joking*, Mike Yarwood published by J. M. Dent. Reprinted by permission of Victor Armour Ltd; HILAIRE BELLOC, 'Grandmama's Birthday' from *Letters from Hilaire Belloc* edited by Robert Speaight published by Hollis & Carter. Reprinted by permission of A. D. Peters & Co. Ltd; TERESA BLOOMINGDALE, excerpt from *'Murphy Must Have Been a Mother'*. Copyright © 1982 by Teresa Bloomingdale. Reprinted by permission of Doubleday, Inc.; LESLIE BRICUSSE, 'When I look in your eyes' from *Doctor Dolittle*. Reprinted by permission of The Big 3, Music/CBS Songs Ltd, 37 Soho Square, London W1; LEONARD CLARK, 'Cowslips' from *Collected Poems and Verses for Children*, published by Dobson Books Ltd; JOHN CUNLIFFE, 'Orders of the Day' from *2nd Poetry Book*, compiled by John Foster, published by Oxford University Press; WALTER DE LA MARE, 'The Cupboard'. Reprinted by permission of the Literary Trustees of Walter de la Mare and The Society of Authors as their representative; SYDNEY FOXCROFT, article from *Sunday People*. Reprinted by permission of Syndication International; PATSY GRAY, essay originally published in *PTA Magazine*, USA; ELIZABETH JENNINGS, 'Old Woman' from *A Sense of the World* published by André Deutsch. Reprinted by permission of David Higham Associates Ltd; SHEILA KITZINGER, excerpts from *Women as Mothers* published by Fontana Paperbacks. Reprinted by permission of publisher; GORDON LORENZ, 'There's no one quite like Grandma'. Copyright © 1980 by EMI Music Publishing Ltd. Reproduced by permission of EMI Music Publishing Ltd and International Music Publications; NORMAN MacCAIG, 'Grandchild' from *Tree of Strings*. Reprinted by permission of Chatto & Windus; HARRY McMAHAN, 'What is a Grandmother?' from *Grandma was Quite a Girl* by Harry and Gloria McMahan, Escondido, California; ELIZABETH MASLEN, 'A Visit to Grannie' from *Treble Poets 1*. Reprinted by permission of Chatto & Windus; CHARLES AND ANN MORSE, excerpts from *Let this be a day for Grandparents*. Reprinted by permission of Saint Mary's Press; PENNY PERRICK, 'There's no limit to the power of a granny' from *The Sun*, 9th November 1977. Reprinted by permission of London Express News and Feature Services; KUSHA PETTS, 'Old Mrs Bodfan's Dance', from *Necklace for a Poor Sod*. Reprinted by permission of Gomer Press; MARJORIE PROOPS, article from the *Sunday Mirror* March 1975. Reprinted by permission of Syndication International Ltd; JOHN PURSER, 'In Memory of Mainie Jellett', from *The Counting Stick* © 1976, Aquila Publishing Co., Isle of Skye; BARBARA REYNOLDS, excerpt from *Jesse Jackson: The Man, The Movement, The Myth* published by Nelson-Hall Inc.; BERTRAND RUSSELL, excerpt from *The Autobiography of Bertrand Russell* published by George, Allen & Unwin; GEORGE SAND, extract from *Lelia, the Life of George Sand*. Copyright André Maurois 1953. Reprinted by permission of Curtis Brown and the André Maurois Estate; JAMES SIMMONS, 'To My Grandmother' from *The Selected James Simmons* published by The Blackstaff Press; THE SUN, excerpt reprinted from *The Sun*, August 26th 1972; HILARY THOMAS, excerpt and illustration from *Grandmother Extraordinary* published by Stewart Williams Publishers. Reprinted by

brought me neither infirmity nor lowered vitality.

Can I still make myself useful? That one may legitimately ask, and I think that I can answer 'yes'. I feel that I may be useful in a more personal, more direct way than ever before. I have, though how I do not know, acquired much wisdom. I am better equipped to bring up children. . . . It is quite wrong to think of old age as a downward slope. One climbs higher and higher with the advancing years, and that, too, with surprising strides.

How good life is when all that one loves is aswarm with life!

George Sand, from a letter to a friend

LOOKING BACK

After I reached the age of fourteen, my grandmother's intellectual limitations became trying to me, and her Puritan morality began to seem to me to be excessive; but while I was a child her great affection for me, and her intense care for my welfare, made me love her and gave me that feeling of safety that children need. I remember when I was about four or five years old lying awake thinking how dreadful it would be when my grandmother was dead. When she did in fact die, which was after I was married, I did not mind at all. But in retrospect, as I have grown older, I have realized more and more the importance she had in moulding my outlook on life. Her fearlessness, her public spirit, her contempt for convention, and her indifference to the opinion of the majority have always seemed good to me and have impressed themselves upon me as worthy of imitation.

Bertrand Russell

or watch his castles fall, unravel
the mysteries of war and space,
patient to watch his feats, and marvel,
bear impudence and carelessness.

More pomp and power goes with a crown;
but, dear, you too gave all you had,
and much more humbly you stepped down,
Not envious, not wishful: glad.

This happier story has no madness
and no ingratitude, no storm,
only its own bearable sadness
here where it is still warm.

James Simmons

TO MY GRANDMOTHER
(while reading 'King Lear')

The laws that rule us all are blind
and powerful and deaf to petition.
They weakened your body and your mind
and put you in King Lear's position.

Now you need more than you can buy,
your married daughters must elect,
gladly and understanding why,
to offer service and respect

without being asked or more rewarded,
without resentment, much less hate.
To you all this is accorded
as, without fuss, you abdicate.

With independence gone, you sit
by daughters' fires, now only able
to settle what you're going to knit:
your chair won't dominate the table.

That king learnt how to serve his clown;
a grandchild lets you be of use:
gladly you put your knitting down
to read to him or hear his views,

GRANDCHILD

She stumbles upon every day
as though it were a four-leaf clover
ringed in a horseshoe.

The light is her luck – and its thickening
into chair, postman, poodle
with a ribbon round its neck.

She plays among godsends
and becomes one. Watch her being
a seal or a sleepy book.

Yet sometimes she wakes in the night
terrified, staring
at somewhere else.

She's learning that ancestors
refuse to be dead. Their resurrection
is her terror.

We soothe the little godsend
back to us
and pray, despairingly –

May the clover be
a true prophet. May her light be
without history.

Norman MacCaig

(The divorce rate is about 50 per cent of all marriages.)

The grandmother's power is also institution-alized in the Caribbean, where grandmothers frequently rear their grandchildren from the time they are weaned.

. . . As the grandmother ages the girls gradually take over more and more responsibility for the running of the household, and by old age a woman expects granddaughters to be caring for her in her turn. It is thought to be a dreadful thing to leave old women without young people to help them, and when I was doing my own field work I interviewed in two households where it was claimed by proud grandmothers that young men who were emigrating had deliberately impregnated girl-friends so that there would be a baby to leave with their mothers when they left. So in some cases the father's and not only the mother's mother also rears grandchildren.

Sheila Kitzinger

A three generation family in Hong Kong

. . . In Atjeh, on the northern tip of Sumatra, women own the houses, and even where men own the land, the women work it. . . . The tie between a mother and her children and grandchildren is the most powerful in the community, and husbands are treated as guests who often outstay their welcome.

coming to any important decision. Thus the Kgatla grandmother is a person with dignity, responsibility, a continuing stake in her children's and grandchildren's progress and welfare, and through her children's fertility has work to do and an established place in society recognized by all.

Worldwide it is quite probable that nearly as many children are brought up by their grandmothers as by their mothers.

In pre-industrial societies the role of the grandmother is frequently of major importance, and it is often not until a woman becomes a grandmother that she attains full dignity and authority as a woman, can speak as an elder, have a hand in the cultural traditions of her people, and represent a value system to her daughters and daughters-in-law. A peak point in a woman's life is when she becomes a grandmother or matriarch. The Chinese veneration for old people is well known. Traditionally, a son's most important obligation is to ensure that his parents have a happy and comfortable old age, and elderly people are afforded something approaching reverence.

The same respect for age exists throughout Africa. Among the Kgatla of Bechuanaland . . . It is the responsibility of married sons to assist their parents with the ploughing, to give them occasional presents and help them in any way they can, whereas married daughters help particularly with gifts of food and clothing and help in the household. There is a great emphasis in honouring and obeying parents, and young people consult them before embarking on any new venture or

TENDER LOVING CARE

My granddaughter is two and takes good care of
   me,
gives me the spectacles I just took off,
insists I drink the abandoned cup of tea,
fetches her linctus for my smoker's cough,
runs in to get the book I meant to leave behind,
orders me off to have an after dinner nap.
She's loving, thoughtful, orderly and kind.
God help her husband, poor beloved chap.

Pam Brown

COWSLIPS

After primroses, cowslips;
I like the name.
Born overnight in open fields
with new grass, first buttercups;
friends of the clay, they have a secret look.
Their heads catch the sun's gold,
dew pearls roll among crinkled leaves,
bees dust probing tongues in honeyed tubes.

My grandmother loved these flowers,
her mother, too, with the long apron strings,
gathered bunches in these same fields
for winter wine, syrups and creams;
I inherit them now, pick a hundred at a time,
make them into tight balls, as they did,
cowslip balls to hang about the thatched house,
smelling of orange and lemon,
pomanders in spring.

Leonard Clark

To become a grandmother is to be suddenly piercingly aware of the brevity of human life. Only the day before yesterday and I was trailing behind my parents, poking in ditches, chivvying ants, calling 'Wait for me!'

Only yesterday I came home in the clapped-out Morris, a shawl-swathed wrinkled red face in the crook of my arm, puckered against the unfamiliar sky.

And now, here is a face so like that other – but another generation, another step into unknown centuries.

That young couple I trotted behind have walked away into shadow. I recall them so vividly that it seems impossible I cannot share this new child with them – and I relive their loss. As they must have yearned for their lost and recollected parents when I myself was born, and my children in their turn.

We are old. We are young. The child, still calling 'Wait for me!' touches for a little while the life of this other child. How strange that it should think me old, should even call me Grandmother.

How strange that this small, helpless thing will stand one day, astonishingly soon, where I now stand, and wonder where those past, bright summers went. As every grandma has since time began.

Every generation whispers its urgent message in

the children's ears – 'Savour every moment. Learn.
Live. Create. Reach out your arms. Look about
you. You have so little time.' And every child smiles
– for it knows it has all time at its disposal and that it
will not, cannot, fail.

Charlotte Gray

IN MEMORY OF MAINIE JELLETT

You died the year that I was born
and so I claim no more than kinship;
yet this sketch in oils – some corn-stooks,
sea, the hills, the shallow glow
of threatened sunlight sixty years
ago: I saw these only yesterday
in this same place; the sheaves
(still sheaves) still gathered in by hand
and fed entire to the beasts – this sketch

brings you alive, perhaps as you were then,
intense as that blue band of sea.
Were your tears then more salt,
or did your blood run wild and brackish
as the sea runs in the Hebrides,
and was this painting how you smoothed
such troubled waters?
    Fresh on this board
and through your eye in mine
they glisten still.

John Purser

OLD WOMAN

So much she caused she cannot now account for
As she stands watching day return, the cool
Walls of the house moving towards the sun.
She puts some flowers in a vase and thinks

  'There is not much I can arrange
In here and now, but flowers are suppliant

As children never were. And love is now
A flicker of memory, my body is
My own entirely. When I lie at night
I gather nothing now into my arms,

  No child or man, and where I live
Is what remains when men and children go.'

Yet she owns more than residue of lives
That she has marked and altered. See how she
Warns time from too much touching her possessions

  By keeping flowers fed by polishing

   Her fine old silver. Gratefully
She sees her own glance printed on grandchildren.

Drawing the curtains back and opening windows
Every morning now, she feels her years
Grow less and less. Time puts no burden on
Her now she does not need to measure it.

  It is acceptance she arranges
And her own life she places in the vase.

            Elizabeth Jennings

Grandparents are to be thanked
for changing a child's fear of old age
into a thing of strange beauty.
It happens with the grandparent
who gives a child tasty things to eat
or who shows the child old and worn treasures
or who knows how to touch a child as he awakens.
Grandparents are to be thanked
for showing a child,
at the beginning of life,
the gentleness of the end of life.

A parent can give a child the stuff of reality;
but a grandparent can clothe that reality
with feelings which make it desirable.
A grandparent's special vision
may not be to see a new world.
But he can know that the old world was good.
And in himself he can reconcile the old and the new.
That is a vision worth sharing.

Grandparents will be thanked
for what they have spoken
and for what they have kept to themselves.
The discoveries they have kept silent about,
leaving the child to find his own.
The dreams, the mistakes, the doubts,
the worries, and the fears of old age
they share only carefully with the young.

Yet without these burdens shared,
none has a chance to grow old gracefully.
Grandparents are to be thanked
for trying anything new,
for the courage to retire
and begin again.

Charles and Ann Morse

I CAN ANSWER 'YES'

July 5th, 1868: Today I have completed sixty-four Springtimes . . . And now here I am, a very old woman, embarked on my sixty-fifth year. By one of those strange oddities in my destiny, I am now in much better health, much stronger, much more active, than I ever was in my youth. . . . I am troubled by no hankering after the days of my youth: I am no longer ambitious for fame: I desire no money except insofar as I should like to be able to leave something to my children and grandchildren. . . . This astonishing old age . . . has

WE'RE ALL IN THIS TOGETHER

They are all of them kind,
patting these hands that are not mine
and promising me tea
Yet do not understand my mind
is clear as theirs
and still the quintessential me
– the child, the lover, good companion, friend.
This end
is my beginning still.
Oh, I am old and ill
– agreed.
But that's the weary flesh, the drab disguise
I'm forced to wear.
Only the children peer into my eyes
and read the truth:
They see
age is a lie
and we are all contemporary.

Pam Brown